I0011944

Table Of Contents

Chapter 1: Introduction to AI in Retail

The Evolution of AI in Retail

The evolution of AI in retail has been nothing short of revolutionary, transforming the way businesses interact with customers and manage their inventory. AI-powered tools have become essential in the retail industry, offering solutions for dynamic pricing, in-store customer tracking, and automated inventory replenishment. These technologies have significantly improved operational efficiency and customer satisfaction, resulting in increased sales and reduced costs for retailers.

One of the most exciting applications of AI in retail is the development of virtual shopping assistants that provide personalized product recommendations to customers. These AI-driven assistants utilize machine learning algorithms to analyze customer behavior and preferences, helping retailers tailor their offerings to individual needs. Additionally, AI-powered chatbots are being used for instant customer support and feedback, enhancing the overall shopping experience for consumers.

Predictive analytics is another key area where AI is making a significant impact in retail. By leveraging AI algorithms, retailers can optimize inventory levels and reduce stockouts, ensuring that they always have the right products in stock to meet customer demand. Automated store layout optimization is also possible with AI, allowing retailers to maximize space and improve the overall shopping experience for customers.

Customer sentiment analysis is another powerful application of AI in retail, enabling businesses to target their marketing campaigns more effectively. By analyzing customer feedback and social media data, retailers can gain valuable insights into consumer preferences and tailor their messaging accordingly. Additionally, AI-powered image recognition technology is being used for seamless checkout and inventory management, streamlining the purchasing process for customers.

In conclusion, the evolution of AI in retail is reshaping the industry in profound ways. From personalized product recommendations to optimized inventory management, AI-powered tools are helping retailers improve customer satisfaction and drive sales. As technology continues to advance, the possibilities for AI in retail are endless, offering new opportunities for businesses to enhance the customer experience and stay ahead of the competition.

Benefits of AI in Retail

In retail, AI is transforming the way businesses operate and interact with their customers. One of the key benefits of AI in retail is its ability to revolutionize customer experience. AI-powered tools such as virtual shopping assistants and chatbots are being used to provide personalized product recommendations and instant customer support. This not only enhances the shopping experience for customers but also increases customer satisfaction and loyalty.

Another significant benefit of AI in retail is its impact on inventory management. AI-driven predictive analytics are being used to optimize inventory levels and reduce stockouts, leading to improved operational efficiency and cost savings. Automated inventory replenishment powered by AI algorithms ensures that retailers always have the right products in stock at the right time, minimizing the risk of overstocking or understocking. AI is also being leveraged for store layout optimization, with algorithms analyzing customer behavior and preferences to create a more engaging and efficient shopping environment. By using AI-driven customer sentiment analysis, retailers can target their marketing campaigns more effectively, leading to higher conversion rates and increased sales.

Furthermore, AI-powered image recognition technology is streamlining the checkout process and improving inventory management. This technology enables retailers to quickly and accurately identify products, reducing checkout times and minimizing errors. Additionally, AI-driven fraud detection and prevention tools are being used to secure retail transactions and protect customer data.

Overall, AI is revolutionizing the retail industry by enhancing customer experience, optimizing inventory management, and improving operational efficiency. By leveraging AI-powered tools and technologies, retailers can stay ahead of the competition and meet the evolving needs of their customers in an increasingly digital world.

Overview of AI Applications in Retail

In the fast-paced world of retail, staying ahead of the competition is crucial. Thanks to advancements in artificial intelligence (AI) technology, retailers now have powerful tools at their disposal to revolutionize the customer experience and streamline inventory management processes. AI applications in retail are diverse and multifaceted, offering a wide range of benefits for both retailers and consumers alike.

One of the key areas where AI is making a significant impact in retail is through dynamic pricing. AI-powered algorithms analyze market trends, competitor pricing, and customer behavior in real-time to adjust prices accordingly. This not only helps retailers maximize profits but also ensures that customers are getting the best possible deals. In addition, AI is also being used for in-store customer tracking, allowing retailers to better understand customer behavior and preferences for personalized marketing strategies.

Automated inventory replenishment is another area where AI is proving to be invaluable. By analyzing historical sales data, current inventory levels, and external factors such as weather patterns, AI can accurately predict demand and automatically reorder stock when needed. This helps to reduce stockouts, minimize excess inventory, and ultimately improve operational efficiency.

AI-driven virtual shopping assistants are also becoming increasingly popular in retail. These personalized assistants use AI algorithms to analyze customer data and provide tailored product recommendations. This not only enhances the shopping experience for customers but also increases sales opportunities for retailers. Additionally, AI-powered chatbots are being used for instant customer support and feedback, providing round-the-clock assistance to shoppers and improving overall customer satisfaction.

Predictive analytics is another key application of AI in retail. By analyzing vast amounts of data, AI algorithms can forecast trends, identify patterns, and optimize inventory levels to meet customer demand. This helps retailers to make informed decisions and stay ahead of the competition. Furthermore, AI-powered image recognition technology is being used for seamless checkout processes and inventory management, making the shopping experience more efficient and convenient for customers.

Overall, AI applications in retail are transforming the way businesses operate and interact with customers. From personalized product recommendations to automated inventory replenishment, AI is revolutionizing the retail industry and setting new standards for customer experience and inventory management. By leveraging the power of AI technology, retailers can stay competitive, drive sales, and ultimately enhance the overall shopping experience for consumers.

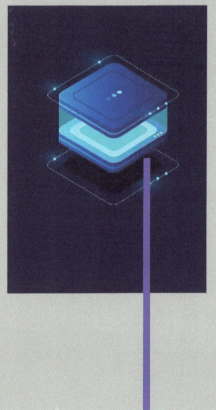

Chapter 2: AI-Powered Tools for Dynamic Pricing

Importance of Dynamic Pricing in Retail

Dynamic pricing in retail is a crucial strategy that can make a significant impact on a company's bottom line. By utilizing artificial intelligence (AI) technology, retailers can adjust prices in real-time based on various factors such as demand, competitor pricing, and inventory levels. This allows retailers to maximize profits by selling products at the right price point at the right time.

One of the key benefits of dynamic pricing is its ability to increase sales and revenue. By setting prices dynamically, retailers can attract price-sensitive customers with lower prices during off-peak hours while maximizing profits during peak times. This flexibility in pricing helps retailers stay competitive in the market and capture more sales opportunities.

Moreover, dynamic pricing can also help retailers optimize inventory levels and reduce stockouts. By analyzing historical sales data and current market trends, AI-powered dynamic pricing tools can predict demand for specific products and adjust prices accordingly to prevent overstocking or understocking. This not only helps retailers save on storage costs but also ensures that customers can find the products they want when they visit the store.

In addition, dynamic pricing can also enhance the overall customer experience. By offering personalized discounts and promotions based on individual customer preferences and behavior, retailers can create a more engaging shopping experience that fosters customer loyalty and repeat purchases. This level of personalization can help retailers build stronger relationships with their customers and differentiate themselves from competitors.

Overall, dynamic pricing powered by AI technology is a game-changer for retailers looking to stay ahead in an increasingly competitive market. By leveraging real-time data and predictive analytics, retailers can optimize pricing strategies, improve operational efficiency, and ultimately drive growth and profitability. As AI continues to revolutionize the retail industry, dynamic pricing will play a crucial role in shaping the future of retail.

AI Algorithms for Dynamic Pricing

AI algorithms for dynamic pricing play a crucial role in the retail industry, allowing businesses to adjust prices in real-time based on various factors such as demand, competitor pricing, and customer behavior. These algorithms analyze large amounts of data to determine the optimal pricing strategy that maximizes profits while remaining competitive in the market. By leveraging AI-powered dynamic pricing tools, retailers can stay ahead of the competition and maximize their revenue potential.

In addition to dynamic pricing, AI-powered tools are also used for in-store customer tracking and automated inventory replenishment. By tracking customer behavior in real-time, retailers can gain valuable insights into customer preferences and shopping patterns, allowing them to personalize the shopping experience and improve customer satisfaction. Automated inventory replenishment ensures that retailers always have the right products in stock, reducing the risk of stockouts and lost sales. These AI-driven solutions significantly improve operational efficiency and help retailers better meet the needs of their customers.

AI-driven virtual shopping assistants are another innovative technology that is revolutionizing the retail industry. These virtual assistants use AI algorithms to provide personalized product recommendations based on customer preferences and purchase history. By leveraging AI-powered chatbots for instant customer support and feedback, retailers can provide a seamless shopping experience and improve customer satisfaction. These AI-driven solutions not only enhance the customer experience but also help retailers streamline their operations and increase sales.

Furthermore, AI-based predictive analytics are being used to optimize inventory levels and reduce stockouts. By analyzing historical sales data, market trends, and other factors, retailers can accurately forecast demand and adjust their inventory levels accordingly. Automated store layout optimization using AI algorithms helps retailers maximize sales by strategically placing products in high-traffic areas. AI-driven customer sentiment analysis allows retailers to target their marketing campaigns more effectively, while AI-powered image recognition technology streamlines checkout processes and inventory management.

Overall, AI is transforming the retail industry in numerous ways, from personalized product recommendations and instant customer support to optimized inventory management and targeted marketing campaigns. By leveraging AI algorithms for dynamic pricing and other innovative technologies, retailers can improve operational efficiency, increase customer satisfaction, and drive revenue growth. As AI continues to advance, its impact on the retail industry will only continue to grow, revolutionizing the way retailers interact with customers and manage their inventory.

Case Studies of Successful Dynamic Pricing Strategies

Dynamic pricing is a strategy that involves adjusting the prices of products or services in real-time based on various factors such as demand, competitor pricing, and inventory levels. In the retail industry, dynamic pricing has become increasingly popular as it allows retailers to maximize profits and stay competitive in today's fast-paced market. In this subchapter, we will explore some case studies of successful dynamic pricing strategies implemented by leading retailers using AI-powered tools.

One example of a successful dynamic pricing strategy is Amazon's use of AI algorithms to adjust prices on millions of products multiple times a day. By analyzing customer behavior, competitor pricing, and inventory levels, Amazon is able to optimize prices to maximize profits while remaining competitive in the market. This has allowed Amazon to increase sales and customer satisfaction while staying ahead of the competition.

Another successful case study is Walmart's use of AI-powered tools for dynamic pricing in its online and offline stores. By analyzing customer data, market trends, and competitor pricing, Walmart is able to adjust prices in real-time to attract more customers and increase sales. This has helped Walmart to improve operational efficiency and drive revenue growth in a highly competitive retail market.

Furthermore, Best Buy has also implemented dynamic pricing strategies using AI-powered tools to adjust prices based on factors such as demand, seasonality, and inventory levels. By analyzing customer data and market trends, Best Buy is able to offer personalized pricing to customers, leading to increased sales and customer loyalty. This has helped Best Buy to stay competitive in the market and drive revenue growth.

Overall, these case studies demonstrate the power of AI in revolutionizing dynamic pricing strategies in the retail industry. By leveraging AI-powered tools for real-time pricing adjustments, retailers can optimize profits, improve customer satisfaction, and stay ahead of the competition in today's fast-paced market. For people that want a comprehensive guide on how to implement successful dynamic pricing strategies using AI in retail, this subchapter provides valuable insights and best practices to help retailers drive revenue growth and customer loyalty.

Chapter 3: AI in Customer Experience

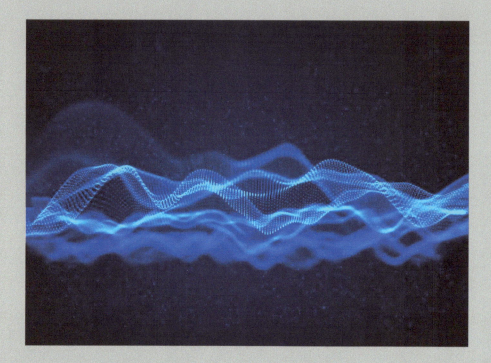

AI-Driven Virtual Shopping Assistants

In retail, AI-driven virtual shopping assistants have become a game-changer in providing personalized product recommendations to customers. These virtual assistants use artificial intelligence algorithms to analyze customer data, browsing history, and purchase behavior to suggest relevant products and services. By leveraging machine learning and natural language processing, these virtual shopping assistants can engage with customers in a more personalized and interactive way, enhancing the overall shopping experience.

Moreover, AI-powered chatbots are being increasingly used in retail for instant customer support and feedback. These chatbots are programmed to respond to customer queries, provide product information, and even process orders in a quick and efficient manner. By harnessing the power of AI, retailers can offer round-the-clock customer service, improving customer satisfaction and loyalty. Additionally, AI-based predictive analytics are being employed to optimize inventory levels and reduce stockouts. By analyzing historical sales data, market trends, and external factors, retailers can forecast demand more accurately, ensuring that the right products are available at the right time.

Furthermore, automated store layout optimization using AI algorithms is transforming the way retailers design their physical spaces. By analyzing foot traffic patterns, customer behavior, and sales data, AI algorithms can recommend optimal store layouts that drive more sales and enhance the overall shopping experience. Additionally, AI-driven customer sentiment analysis is being used for targeted marketing campaigns. By analyzing social media feeds, customer reviews, and feedback, retailers can gain valuable insights into customer preferences and sentiments, enabling them to tailor marketing messages and promotions accordingly.

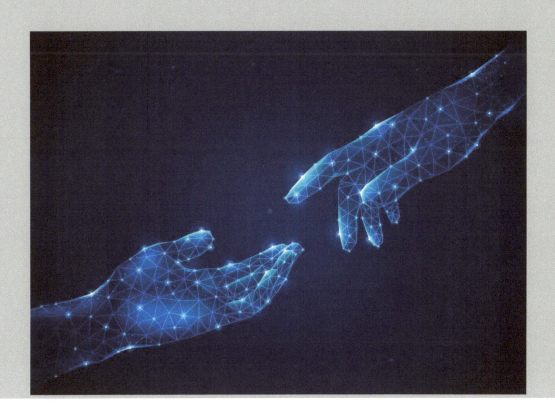

AI-powered image recognition technology is also revolutionizing the checkout process and inventory management in retail stores. By using computer vision algorithms, retailers can automatically identify products, track inventory levels, and even detect fraudulent activities at checkout. This not only streamlines operations but also enhances the overall shopping experience for customers. Moreover, AI-powered fraud detection and prevention tools are being deployed to safeguard retail transactions. By analyzing transaction data in real-time, AI algorithms can detect suspicious activities and prevent fraudulent transactions, protecting both retailers and customers from financial losses.

Lastly, AI-driven supply chain management is enabling real-time inventory tracking and replenishment. By leveraging AI algorithms, retailers can optimize their supply chain operations, reduce lead times, and ensure that products are available when and where they are needed. Additionally, AI-driven customer segmentation is helping retailers to personalize their marketing strategies. By analyzing customer data and behavior, retailers can identify distinct customer segments and tailor their marketing messages and promotions to target specific groups effectively. Furthermore, AI-powered recommendation engines are being used to identify cross-selling and upselling opportunities in retail stores. By analyzing customer data and purchase history, retailers can recommend complementary products and services to customers, increasing sales and customer satisfaction.

AI-Powered Chatbots for Customer Support

AI-powered chatbots are transforming the way retail businesses handle customer support. These chatbots use artificial intelligence to provide instant responses to customer inquiries and feedback, improving the overall customer experience. By utilizing AI technology, retailers can ensure that their customers receive timely and accurate assistance, leading to higher satisfaction levels and increased loyalty.

One of the key benefits of AI-powered chatbots for customer support is their ability to handle a large volume of inquiries simultaneously. Unlike human agents, chatbots can interact with multiple customers at once, providing real-time assistance around the clock. This not only reduces wait times for customers but also allows businesses to scale their customer support operations without having to hire additional staff.

In addition to providing instant customer support, AI-powered chatbots can also gather valuable feedback from customers. By analyzing the conversations between customers and chatbots, retailers can gain insights into customer preferences, pain points, and trends. This data can then be used to improve products and services, personalize marketing campaigns, and enhance the overall customer experience.

Furthermore, AI-powered chatbots can be programmed to handle a wide range of tasks, from answering frequently asked questions to processing returns and exchanges. This automation of routine customer support tasks frees up human agents to focus on more complex issues and strategic initiatives. As a result, businesses can improve operational efficiency and reduce costs while still delivering high-quality customer service.

Overall, AI-powered chatbots are a valuable tool for retailers looking to revolutionize their customer support operations. By leveraging artificial intelligence technology, businesses can provide instant assistance, gather valuable feedback, automate routine tasks, and improve the overall customer experience. As AI continues to advance, chatbots are poised to become an essential component of any retail business's customer support strategy.

Customer Sentiment Analysis with AI

Customer Sentiment Analysis with AI is a game-changer in the retail industry, allowing businesses to gain valuable insights into customer preferences and behaviors. By using AI algorithms to analyze customer feedback, reviews, and social media interactions, retailers can better understand how customers feel about their products and services. This information can then be used to tailor marketing campaigns, improve customer service, and enhance overall customer satisfaction.

One of the key benefits of Customer Sentiment Analysis with AI is its ability to provide real-time feedback on customer sentiment. By automatically analyzing large volumes of data, retailers can quickly identify trends and patterns in customer feedback, allowing them to respond to issues and concerns in a timely manner. This proactive approach to customer feedback can help businesses build stronger relationships with their customers and improve brand loyalty.

AI-powered tools for Customer Sentiment Analysis can also help retailers identify opportunities for targeted marketing campaigns. By understanding the emotions and preferences of their customers, businesses can create more personalized and relevant marketing messages that resonate with their target audience. This can lead to increased customer engagement, higher conversion rates, and ultimately, increased sales and revenue.

In addition to targeted marketing campaigns, AI-driven Customer Sentiment Analysis can also be used to identify potential areas for improvement in products and services. By analyzing customer feedback and sentiment, retailers can pinpoint areas where they may be falling short and make necessary adjustments to improve customer satisfaction. This data-driven approach to business decision-making can help businesses stay ahead of the competition and drive continuous improvement in customer experience.

Overall, Customer Sentiment Analysis with AI is a powerful tool for retailers looking to revolutionize their customer experience and inventory management strategies. By harnessing the power of AI algorithms to analyze customer sentiment, businesses can gain valuable insights into customer preferences, behaviors, and emotions. This information can then be used to drive targeted marketing campaigns, improve customer service, and enhance overall customer satisfaction, ultimately leading to increased sales and revenue for retail businesses.

Chapter 4: AI in Inventory Management

Automated Inventory Replenishment

Automated Inventory Replenishment is a crucial aspect of modern retail operations that can significantly impact a company's bottom line. By utilizing AI-powered tools, retailers can streamline the replenishment process and ensure that shelves are always stocked with the right products at the right time. This not only improves operational efficiency but also enhances customer satisfaction by reducing stockouts and ensuring that popular items are always available. One of the key benefits of Automated Inventory Replenishment is its ability to optimize inventory levels based on real-time data and predictive analytics. By analyzing sales trends, seasonality, and other factors, AI algorithms can accurately forecast demand and automatically reorder products when inventory levels are low. This proactive approach helps retailers avoid overstocking or understocking issues, ultimately leading to cost savings and improved inventory turnover.

In addition to optimizing inventory levels, AI-powered tools can also automate the process of restocking shelves and managing inventory in the backroom. By using image recognition technology, retailers can quickly identify products that need to be replenished and generate restocking orders with minimal human intervention. This not only saves time and reduces the risk of human error but also ensures that products are always available for customers when they need them.

Furthermore, Automated Inventory Replenishment can be integrated with AI-driven supply chain management systems to enable real-time inventory tracking and replenishment. By connecting with suppliers and logistics partners, retailers can automate the entire replenishment process from order placement to delivery, ensuring that products are restocked efficiently and cost-effectively. This seamless integration of AI technologies allows retailers to optimize their supply chain operations and respond quickly to changing market conditions.

Overall, Automated Inventory Replenishment is a game-changer for retailers looking to improve their operational efficiency and customer satisfaction. By leveraging AI-powered tools for inventory management, retailers can reduce costs, minimize stockouts, and enhance the overall shopping experience for their customers. As technology continues to advance, the possibilities for Automated Inventory Replenishment in retail are endless, making it a must-have tool for any retailer looking to stay ahead in today's competitive market.

AI-Based Predictive Analytics for Inventory Optimization

AI-based predictive analytics for inventory optimization is a game-changer in the retail industry. By leveraging artificial intelligence to analyze historical data and patterns, retailers can make informed decisions about their inventory levels, reducing the risk of stockouts and overstock situations. This not only improves operational efficiency but also enhances customer satisfaction by ensuring that products are always available when needed.

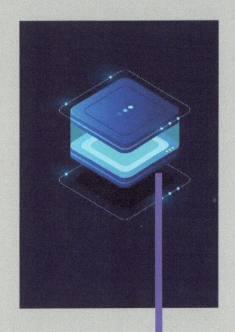

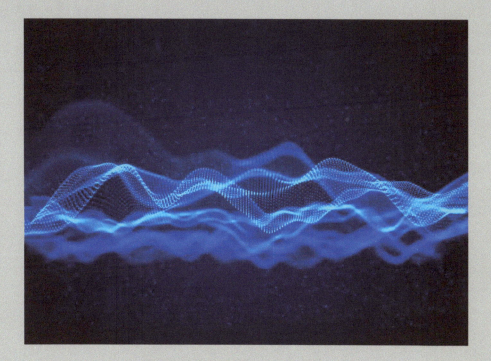

One key benefit of AI-based predictive analytics is its ability to forecast demand accurately. By analyzing factors such as seasonality, trends, and even external events like weather patterns, retailers can optimize their inventory levels to meet customer demand without excess stock. This not only saves costs associated with overstocking but also maximizes sales opportunities by ensuring that popular items are always in stock.

Furthermore, AI-driven predictive analytics can help retailers identify potential supply chain disruptions before they occur. By monitoring data in real-time and predicting potential issues, retailers can take proactive measures to prevent stockouts and delays in product availability. This proactive approach not only saves costs but also ensures a seamless shopping experience for customers.

In addition to optimizing inventory levels, AI-based predictive analytics can also help retailers with store layout optimization. By analyzing customer behavior and preferences, retailers can optimize their store layout to enhance the shopping experience and increase sales. This personalized approach can lead to higher customer satisfaction and loyalty, ultimately driving revenue growth for retailers.

Overall, AI-based predictive analytics for inventory optimization is a powerful tool that can revolutionize the retail industry. By leveraging artificial intelligence to make data-driven decisions, retailers can improve operational efficiency, enhance customer satisfaction, and drive revenue growth. As technology continues to advance, retailers who embrace AI-based predictive analytics will have a competitive edge in the ever-evolving retail landscape.

Store Layout Optimization using AI Algorithms

In the retail industry, the use of Artificial Intelligence (AI) algorithms is revolutionizing the way stores are laid out to optimize the shopping experience for customers. By leveraging AI technology, retailers can analyze customer behavior, preferences, and purchase patterns to create a store layout that maximizes sales and enhances customer satisfaction. AI algorithms can help retailers determine the best placement of products, aisles, and displays to drive traffic flow and increase sales.

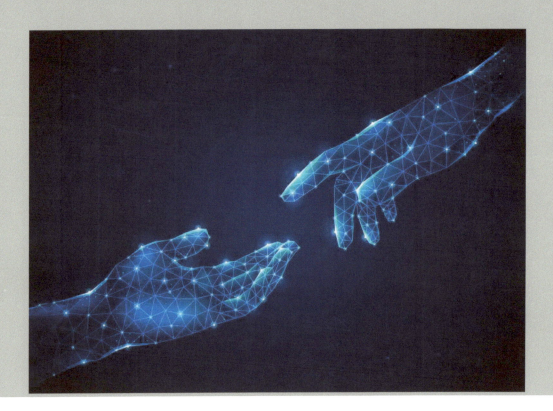

One of the key benefits of using AI algorithms for store layout optimization is the ability to personalize the shopping experience for each customer. By analyzing data on customer demographics, purchasing history, and preferences, retailers can tailor the layout of their stores to meet the specific needs and preferences of individual shoppers. This personalized approach can lead to increased customer loyalty, higher sales conversion rates, and improved overall customer satisfaction.

AI algorithms can also help retailers optimize inventory management by predicting demand, reducing stockouts, and minimizing overstock situations. By analyzing historical sales data, seasonal trends, and external factors such as weather or economic conditions, AI algorithms can provide retailers with valuable insights into how to best allocate inventory across different store locations. This can help retailers reduce costs, improve efficiency, and enhance the overall shopping experience for customers.

Furthermore, AI algorithms can assist retailers in making data-driven decisions about store layout changes and improvements. By analyzing real-time data on customer traffic patterns, dwell times, and engagement levels, retailers can identify areas of their stores that may need adjustment or optimization. This continuous feedback loop can help retailers stay agile and responsive to changing customer needs and preferences, ultimately leading to a more engaging and profitable shopping experience.

Overall, the use of AI algorithms for store layout optimization represents a significant opportunity for retailers to enhance customer experience, drive sales, and improve operational efficiency. By leveraging the power of AI technology, retailers can create personalized, data-driven store layouts that meet the needs and preferences of their customers, ultimately leading to increased satisfaction and loyalty.

Chapter 5: AI in Marketing and Sales

AI-Driven Customer Segmentation

AI-driven customer segmentation is a powerful tool that allows retailers to understand their customers on a deeper level, enabling them to create personalized marketing strategies that cater to individual preferences and behaviors. By harnessing the power of artificial intelligence, retailers can analyze vast amounts of data to identify patterns and trends that can inform targeted marketing campaigns. This level of segmentation goes beyond traditional demographic categories, allowing retailers to target customers based on their shopping habits, preferences, and purchase history.

One of the key benefits of AI-driven customer segmentation is the ability to create personalized shopping experiences for customers. By segmenting customers into groups based on their behavior and preferences, retailers can tailor marketing messages and promotions to resonate with each segment. This not only improves customer satisfaction but also increases the likelihood of repeat purchases and customer loyalty. With AI-driven customer segmentation, retailers can create targeted marketing campaigns that speak directly to the needs and interests of their customers, driving sales and revenue.

In addition to personalized marketing strategies, AI-driven customer segmentation can also help retailers optimize their inventory levels and reduce stockouts. By segmenting customers based on their purchasing behavior, retailers can forecast demand more accurately and ensure that they have the right products in stock at the right time. This can help retailers minimize overstocking and understocking issues, leading to improved operational efficiency and customer satisfaction. By leveraging AI-powered predictive analytics, retailers can optimize their inventory management processes and reduce the risk of lost sales due to stockouts.

Furthermore, AI-driven customer segmentation can also be used to improve the overall customer experience in retail stores. By understanding the preferences and behaviors of different customer segments, retailers can tailor their store layouts and product displays to better meet the needs of their customers. This can lead to a more seamless shopping experience for customers, increasing the likelihood of purchase and customer satisfaction. By using AI algorithms to optimize store layouts, retailers can create a more engaging and personalized shopping environment that encourages customers to spend more time in-store and make more purchases.

Overall, AI-driven customer segmentation is a valuable tool for retailers looking to revolutionize their customer experience and inventory management. By leveraging the power of artificial intelligence, retailers can create personalized marketing strategies, optimize inventory levels, and improve the overall customer experience in their stores. With AI-driven customer segmentation, retailers can stay ahead of the competition and meet the evolving needs and expectations of their customers in the digital age.

AI-Powered Recommendation Engines

AI-powered recommendation engines are a game-changer in the retail industry, providing personalized product recommendations to customers based on their preferences and browsing history. These recommendation engines use machine learning algorithms to analyze customer data and suggest relevant products, increasing the likelihood of a purchase and boosting sales for retailers. By leveraging AI technology, retailers can offer a more tailored shopping experience, leading to higher customer satisfaction and loyalty.

One of the key benefits of AI-powered recommendation engines is their ability to drive cross-selling and upselling opportunities in retail stores. By analyzing customer behavior and purchase history, these engines can suggest complementary products or upgrades to customers, increasing the average order value and maximizing revenue for retailers. This targeted approach not only enhances the shopping experience for customers but also helps retailers increase their bottom line through strategic product recommendations.

In addition to driving sales, AI-powered recommendation engines also play a crucial role in improving inventory management in retail. By analyzing real-time sales data and customer preferences, these engines can help retailers optimize their inventory levels and reduce stockouts. This proactive approach to inventory management ensures that retailers have the right products in stock at the right time, minimizing lost sales opportunities and improving operational efficiency.

Furthermore, AI-powered recommendation engines can also be used to enhance the online shopping experience through personalized product recommendations. By analyzing customer behavior and preferences, these engines can suggest relevant products to customers as they browse an online store, increasing the likelihood of a purchase. This personalized approach to online shopping not only improves customer satisfaction but also helps retailers increase their online conversion rates and drive revenue growth.

Overall, AI-powered recommendation engines are a powerful tool for retailers looking to revolutionize their customer experience and inventory management. By leveraging the latest advancements in AI technology, retailers can provide personalized product recommendations, drive cross-selling and upselling opportunities, optimize inventory levels, and enhance the online shopping experience. As AI continues to transform the retail industry, recommendation engines will play a crucial role in helping retailers stay ahead of the competition and meet the evolving needs of today's consumers.

Targeted Marketing Campaigns with AI

Targeted Marketing Campaigns with AI are revolutionizing the way retailers connect with their customers. By harnessing the power of artificial intelligence, retailers can create personalized and highly targeted marketing campaigns that resonate with their target audience. AI-driven customer segmentation allows retailers to identify different customer groups based on their preferences, behavior, and purchasing patterns. This enables retailers to tailor their marketing messages to each group, increasing the likelihood of conversion and customer loyalty.

One of the key benefits of using AI for targeted marketing campaigns is the ability to analyze customer sentiment in real-time. AI-driven sentiment analysis tools can monitor social media, customer reviews, and other online sources to gauge how customers feel about a brand or product. This valuable information can be used to craft marketing messages that speak directly to customer needs and desires, increasing the effectiveness of marketing campaigns and driving sales.

AI-powered recommendation engines are another powerful tool for targeted marketing campaigns in retail. By analyzing customer data and behavior, recommendation engines can suggest products that are likely to interest individual customers. This not only enhances the shopping experience for customers but also increases the likelihood of cross-selling and upselling opportunities for retailers. By leveraging AI to make personalized product recommendations, retailers can drive higher sales and increase customer satisfaction.

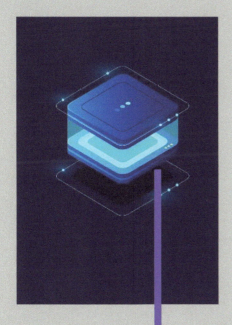

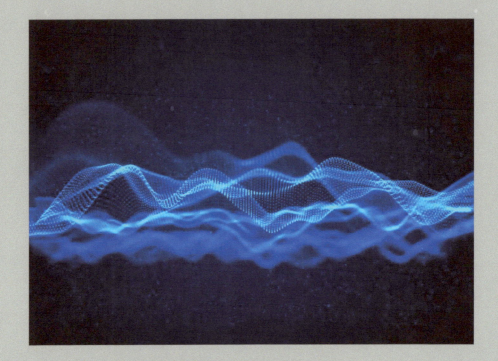

In addition to personalized product recommendations, AI-powered image recognition technology is transforming the checkout process and inventory management in retail stores. By using AI algorithms to recognize products and track inventory levels, retailers can streamline operations and reduce errors. This not only improves efficiency but also enhances the overall customer experience by making checkout faster and more convenient for shoppers.

Overall, targeted marketing campaigns with AI are a game-changer for retailers looking to optimize their marketing strategies and drive sales. By leveraging AI technologies such as customer segmentation, sentiment analysis, recommendation engines, and image recognition, retailers can create highly personalized and effective marketing campaigns that resonate with customers. This not only improves customer satisfaction but also boosts sales and strengthens brand loyalty in an increasingly competitive retail landscape.

Chapter 6: AI in Operations and Security

AI-Powered Image Recognition for Checkout

AI-powered image recognition is revolutionizing the retail industry, particularly in the checkout process. This technology utilizes advanced algorithms to analyze images and identify products quickly and accurately. By implementing AI-powered image recognition at checkout counters, retailers can streamline the payment process and improve overall customer satisfaction. This technology also helps in inventory management by automatically updating stock levels and tracking sales in real-time.

One of the key benefits of AI-powered image recognition for checkout is its ability to reduce human error. Traditional checkout processes often rely on manual scanning of barcodes, which can lead to mistakes and delays. With AI technology, cameras can capture images of products and instantly match them to the correct item in the database, ensuring that the right product is charged accurately. This not only speeds up the checkout process but also improves the overall accuracy of transactions.

Furthermore, AI-powered image recognition can enhance the customer experience by providing a seamless and convenient checkout process. Customers no longer need to search for barcodes or wait for items to be scanned individually. Instead, they can simply place their items on the checkout counter, and the AI system will automatically recognize and ring up each product. This not only saves time but also creates a more efficient and frictionless shopping experience for consumers.

Additionally, AI-powered image recognition can help retailers better manage their inventory levels. By accurately tracking sales and stock levels in real-time, retailers can optimize their replenishment processes and avoid stockouts. This ensures that customers always have access to the products they need and helps retailers maximize their revenue by minimizing lost sales opportunities.

Overall, AI-powered image recognition for checkout is a game-changer for the retail industry. By leveraging advanced technology to streamline the checkout process, retailers can improve operational efficiency, reduce errors, and enhance the overall customer experience. As AI continues to evolve, we can expect to see even more innovative applications of image recognition technology in the retail sector.

Fraud Detection and Prevention with AI

Fraud detection and prevention are critical aspects of retail operations that can significantly impact a company's bottom line. With the rise of online transactions and the increasing sophistication of fraudsters, retailers are turning to artificial intelligence (AI) to help combat fraudulent activities. AI-powered tools are being used to detect and prevent fraud in real-time, helping retailers identify and stop fraudulent transactions before they can cause any financial harm.

One of the key benefits of using AI for fraud detection is its ability to analyze vast amounts of data quickly and accurately. By leveraging machine learning algorithms, AI can identify patterns and anomalies in transaction data that may indicate fraudulent activity. This allows retailers to take immediate action to stop fraudulent transactions and protect their customers' sensitive information.

In addition to detecting fraud in real-time, AI can also help retailers prevent fraudulent activities from occurring in the first place. By using predictive analytics, AI can identify potential fraudsters before they have a chance to carry out their schemes. This proactive approach to fraud prevention can save retailers time and money by preventing fraudulent transactions before they occur.

AI-powered fraud detection and prevention tools can also help retailers improve their overall security posture. By continuously monitoring and analyzing transaction data, AI can identify potential vulnerabilities in a retailer's systems and processes, allowing them to take corrective action to strengthen their defenses against fraudsters.

Overall, AI is revolutionizing fraud detection and prevention in retail by providing retailers with the tools they need to protect their customers and their bottom line. By leveraging the power of AI, retailers can stay one step ahead of fraudsters and ensure that their transactions are secure and trustworthy.

AI-Driven Supply Chain Management

AI-driven supply chain management is a game-changer in the retail industry, allowing businesses to streamline their operations and improve overall efficiency. By utilizing artificial intelligence tools, retailers can achieve real-time inventory tracking and automated inventory replenishment, ensuring that products are always in stock and ready for purchase. This not only reduces the risk of stockouts but also helps businesses optimize their inventory levels and minimize excess stock, ultimately leading to cost savings and improved profitability.

One of the key benefits of AI-driven supply chain management is the ability to track inventory in real-time, providing retailers with valuable insights into their stock levels and product availability. This allows businesses to better plan and forecast their inventory needs, ensuring that they always have the right products on hand to meet customer demand. By automating the replenishment process, retailers can also minimize the risk of overstocking or understocking, resulting in a more efficient and cost-effective supply chain.

In addition to real-time inventory tracking and automated replenishment, AI-driven supply chain management also enables retailers to optimize their supply chain processes and improve overall operational efficiency. By leveraging AI algorithms and predictive analytics, businesses can identify potential bottlenecks in their supply chain, optimize their logistics and distribution networks, and improve the overall flow of goods from suppliers to customers. This not only helps businesses reduce lead times and improve delivery times but also enhances customer satisfaction by ensuring that products are delivered in a timely manner. Furthermore, AI-driven supply chain management can help retailers better understand their customers and tailor their marketing strategies to meet their needs. By utilizing AI-powered customer segmentation tools, businesses can identify different customer segments based on their purchasing behavior, preferences, and demographics. This allows retailers to create personalized marketing campaigns and targeted promotions that resonate with specific customer groups, ultimately leading to increased sales and customer loyalty.

Overall, AI-driven supply chain management is revolutionizing the retail industry by providing businesses with the tools they need to optimize their operations, improve customer satisfaction, and drive profitability. By leveraging artificial intelligence technologies, retailers can achieve real-time inventory tracking, automated replenishment, optimized supply chain processes, and personalized marketing strategies, ultimately transforming the way they do business and enhancing the overall customer experience.

Chapter 7: Conclusion and Future Trends

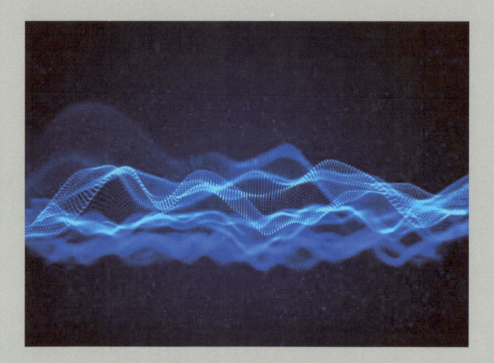

The Future of AI in Retail

The future of AI in retail is bright, with endless possibilities for revolutionizing the customer experience and inventory management. AI-powered tools are already being used in various ways to enhance operational efficiency and customer satisfaction. From dynamic pricing strategies to in-store customer tracking, retailers are finding innovative ways to leverage AI technology.

One of the most exciting developments in AI for retail is the use of virtual shopping assistants. These AI-driven assistants can provide personalized product recommendations based on a customer's browsing history and preferences. This level of personalization can greatly enhance the shopping experience and increase customer loyalty.

Another key application of AI in retail is the use of chatbots for instant customer support and feedback. These AI-powered chatbots can provide real-time assistance to customers, helping to improve customer satisfaction and resolve issues quickly and efficiently. In addition, AI-based predictive analytics are being used to optimize inventory levels and reduce stockouts, ensuring that retailers always have the right products in stock.

AI is also being used to automate store layout optimization, using algorithms to maximize space and improve the flow of customers through the store. This can lead to increased sales and a better overall shopping experience for customers. Additionally, AI-driven customer sentiment analysis is helping retailers to target their marketing campaigns more effectively, ensuring that promotions and advertisements resonate with their target audience.

Overall, the future of AI in retail is promising, with countless opportunities for innovation and growth. From personalized product recommendations to seamless checkout processes, AI is transforming the way retailers do business. By embracing AI technology, retailers can stay ahead of the competition and provide an exceptional shopping experience for their customers.

Implementing AI in Retail Successfully

Implementing AI in retail successfully requires a strategic approach that aligns with the specific needs and goals of the business. One of the key areas where AI is making a significant impact is in dynamic pricing. By leveraging AI-powered tools, retailers can adjust prices in real-time based on factors such as demand, competitor pricing, and inventory levels. This not only helps to maximize profits but also ensures that customers are getting the best possible deals.

In-store customer tracking is another area where AI is revolutionizing the retail experience. By using AI-powered systems to monitor customer behavior and preferences, retailers can tailor their offerings to better meet the needs of their customers. This can lead to increased customer satisfaction and loyalty, as well as higher sales and profits. Automated inventory replenishment is also a crucial aspect of AI implementation in retail. By using AI algorithms to predict demand and automatically reorder products when inventory levels are low, retailers can avoid stockouts and ensure that customers always have access to the products they want.

AI-driven virtual shopping assistants are becoming increasingly popular in retail, as they provide personalized product recommendations based on customer preferences and behavior. This not only enhances the shopping experience but also increases sales by guiding customers towards products that are more likely to interest them. Similarly, AI-powered chatbots are being used for instant customer support and feedback, providing customers with quick and efficient assistance whenever they need it.

AI-based predictive analytics is another powerful tool for retailers, as it allows them to optimize inventory levels and reduce stockouts by forecasting demand more accurately. By analyzing historical data and trends, retailers can make more informed decisions about what products to stock and when to reorder them. Automated store layout optimization using AI algorithms is also gaining traction in retail, as it helps retailers to design their store layouts in a way that maximizes sales and enhances the overall shopping experience for customers.

Case Studies of AI Transformation in Retail

In the subchapter "Case Studies of AI Transformation in Retail," we will delve into real-world examples of how artificial intelligence is revolutionizing the retail industry. These case studies provide insights into the practical applications of AI in enhancing customer experience and optimizing inventory management. By examining these successful implementations, readers can gain a deeper understanding of the potential benefits and challenges of integrating AI technologies into their own retail operations.

One compelling case study involves the use of AI-powered tools for dynamic pricing in a major retail chain. By leveraging machine learning algorithms to analyze market trends and consumer behavior in real-time, the retailer was able to adjust prices dynamically to maximize profitability while remaining competitive. This not only improved sales and margins but also enhanced customer satisfaction by offering competitive pricing. Another case study showcases the implementation of AI-driven virtual shopping assistants for personalized product recommendations in an online retail platform. By utilizing natural language processing and machine learning algorithms, the virtual assistant was able to understand customer preferences and provide tailored product recommendations, leading to increased conversion rates and customer engagement. This personalized shopping experience not only improved customer satisfaction but also increased average order value.

Furthermore, a case study on AI-powered chatbots for instant customer support and feedback highlights the importance of leveraging AI technologies to enhance customer service in retail. By deploying chatbots equipped with natural language processing capabilities, a retailer was able to provide instant responses to customer queries, resolve issues efficiently, and gather valuable feedback for continuous improvement. This not only reduced response times and operational costs but also enhanced overall customer experience.

Additionally, a case study on AI-based predictive analytics for optimizing inventory levels and reducing stockouts demonstrates the significant impact of AI on inventory management in retail. By analyzing historical sales data, market trends, and other relevant factors, a retailer was able to predict demand accurately, optimize inventory levels, and reduce instances of stockouts. This not only improved operational efficiency and reduced carrying costs but also enhanced customer satisfaction by ensuring product availability.

In conclusion, these case studies illustrate the transformative power of AI in retail, showcasing how AI technologies can drive operational efficiency, enhance customer experience, and optimize inventory management. By learning from these real-world examples and understanding the key principles behind successful AI implementations in retail, readers can gain valuable insights into how AI can revolutionize their own retail operations for improved profitability and customer satisfaction.